A Cranic
of Ordinaries

also by Eliza O'Toole

The Dropping of Petals

A Cranic
of Ordinaries

(the light was like light in a Constable painting)

Eliza O'Toole

Shearsman Books

First published in the United Kingdom in 2024 by
Shearsman Books Ltd
PO Box 4239
Swindon
SN3 9FN

Shearsman Books Ltd Registered Office
30–31 St. James Place, Mangotsfield, Bristol BS16 9JB
(this address not for correspondence)

www.shearsman.com

ISBN 978-1-84861-927-2

Contents

For Fin, the best of collaborators, best of companions.

"The day was green"

—Wallace Stevens

Usual is wind from the east

(winter aconite, reaction to light, endogenous rhythms)

It was a machine gun of a morning, a cock pheasant in a clamour of flight and a woodpecker jack-hammering. The sky was green. It was astringent and the blackthorn was wild and white. It was the way the oak was growing, narrowing the sky and fracture-pruned. It was stag-headed and rose over. The kites were cork screwing, a pair, slowly circling way up there. Fin was mesmerised. Then it started to sleet, and there was a vast inrolling of petals and ice was in the air. It was a capitulum of a closing after the beginning of an opening, it was loss of light intensity and temperature drop. It was *eranthis hyemalis*, cowled and hooded, ground-hugging and glowing, bane butter yellow-spilling, arisen from a mythological dog's vomiting.

Stour Owls

The dark comes up from the land to meet
the call of the tawny owl and the tang of
just crushed wild sage. Damp soil and
holm oaks surround. She calls in the
gloam ahead and to the left from the
bronchial tracery of the dead chestnut.
There's no movement, not a breath, no
wind. Her calls increase in frequency and
in pitch. And to the right, a slight pin-thin
hoot. He's located her and then there's
silence so deep we hear the sky sigh. And
then the low slow of the barn owl as the
white slide of her glide brushes the air we
both hold & then breathe.

the colours of pollen

(put pollen upon for the sake of fertilisation)

It was a vixen-piss of a morning. Sour scat of that. A brace of pink-legged partridge startle. Fin, scenting, nose to the ground finds shreds of pelt, scatterings of barbes and down, moults of winter coat windblown and then tiny white sharp shucked knuckles, links of vertebrae laid down slight covered in copper curls of last year's slow-stuck wet dehiscing leaves. And in the blet scent of that Fin, rootling under the cherry plum, flushes a blackbird and they both jump, dusting a blush of brick-red pollen brightly onto bone.

It was the way the light was falling

(unfastening, west of the horse shoe weir)

It faltered, a rainy river morning, gravid with sleet. And in the shul shul of the wind, black-backed gulls were sliding. And in the fret and mute and the slap of that, a twisted thing. Hand, eye and Fin, bolt upright. In the sough and creep, the lifting and the withdrawing, a scuppering. Overwhelmed, strip-barked, part skinned, eyes gone, sinews skeined. Plundered. Catched, coagulating, fractured branches, hedge-whacked twigs, plastic sacking, renegade baling twine (blue), snare-tight Alder root snatch-ravelling rib bones and then unmooring. A pruning. Creely the riverbank, the colour of cold, it was the crows, the crows, the sky as thin as tin and in the sedge, Fin quivering.

Unearthed

(stræl, belonging to a bow, a splintering)

At dawn, a tawny owl was calling. It was that sort of morning. Fin was watching contrails split the sky. It was greening, a wild garlic of a morning, emerald and styptic white and the plough lines, pitch perfect, were reaching right into the sky.

It was the way the barley was breaking through, the way the barleybirds rose in a single motion, the way the moon was transparently there, like a marble in my mouth. And it was the way the field was overturned, belly-sown with knuckles of bone, spicules of silicious stone, cortical dorsal and newly arisen. Fin was digging wriggling in the earth, warm brown musky aroma of dirt arced & showering. It was flicked up, hard-hammer struck, then a chip and then a splinter, it was shot, it was lithic, and then it was an echo of a relic of an elf-arrow head.

Then ascending, it was the way the horizon was perched pigeon-feather soft, fine-bladed with flakes of cloud and squat colours of flint, scattered, and as our track ditched the burgage plot, there was strong green through old stone, and it was growing over.

In the cold, the air was thickening.

A mycorrhizal mourning

matted and lore, the oak loaming, the sky cerulean blue. The spore scent of tin, canker, cord wood tannin. A yolk egg-yellow crocus poking. On the upstroke, a keel bone turns on the thermals, she rises with the sun, soaring on the updraft, a fox-red glint high in the sky. Dihedral. Fin nudges me and drops a dunnock in my hand. Stopped. Soft. Mute chestnut, flecked, grey down, the rib cages an acorn. Cupped in my hand, the head lolls. Eyes closed. Tarsals like twigs. Stalled on the wing, precision at speed, wishbone broken. An instant. Prey dropped for the catch. Teaching her young to sing. Fin waits, he's watching the kite circle, his neck is craned. He's waiting for the sky to rain again tiny warm silent birds.

Scare crows, it was a blæc death, it was a murder

(as the crow flies)

It was a shock. Not a gas gun stunning
of the morning, raising riots of wood
pigeons clap-cracking & clacking, not
warping our walking, not making us
run. It was a sudden blow, we were
shred and thrown, stopped fast and
in the cleaving rain, we stood heaped
as sheaves, one against the other. In
a shock, still. It was feather-dark,
absorbing all the light, it was a sweart
swinging thing. Blacker than Fin, and
leaning in, he was shivering. And
then there were rows. They were slight
winging buffetings spread across the
harrowed fields, they were striking,
and, on the horizon, it was a slap and
a punch, they were hanging there,
swinging there, they were crucified
there, they were spreadeagling and
cable-tied, fletching, gibbeting and
wind-fidgeting there. They were
strong-beaked and silent, they were
scaring, they were sown and broken,
and they had been grackle-glossy
black clever carrion crows.

The closure of crocus
(Crocus is an example of a flower that closes when temperatures drop. Colour is withheld. The possibility of pollination too. The minimum decrease in temperature … [is] … about equal to the temperature rise required for opening.)

It was an owl call of a morning, cold and fey. Ice-tipped rigid immobility, a white day.

Specere – to look at, to see, behold

("The particular thing among many to which the looks are turned.")

There's a sharp dry. Under the blue
sky the tilth-rib rolled is flat and matt
and in the edge of the ditch, still there
are dog violets and prim(e)rose. It was
a tang of a morning, a hush and then
a single song thrush.

It was dusk

The sun was going down. A lone bombelyn humbled hound grass. Fin was growling at the rising moon. Full, fat, tangerine. About to crest the craze of birches, swaying slightly, the moonlight bright. Pioneering. The tawny owls were calling, back and forth. The plough was shearing the sky and the valley was resounding. It was percussive. A vixen was screaming. It was February and the witch-hazel was silent. A foot above the ground, in a ghost of feather-wing white, a barn owl glanced aslant in full flight. The sky was high. And the scent of the dog violets was obsidian. Spring was shivering.

Tread depth, earth gazing
(first there was a garden, then there was a fall, then there was farming)

And in the light of that moment of truth, I saw dandelions and daisies, I saw reverting roses. And then when the song thrush sang, I saw the field was just flush with first green, edged with bare wood bursting, with cherry plum and blackthorn blossom, with catkins long and lemon, gold-velvet and grey, and hard by the hazed lattice of thrashed hedge brush, under the 50mill tread of a *goodyear* tyre (*serial number 540/65R24*) there were shoots of cuckoo barley and flowers of nobody's gardens going wild.

Jackdaw trees

(worm trails and thaw calling up daffodils in the season of sowing barley)

Jackdaws this evening like leaves
filling out winter trees, and in
between long thin sharp shadows
filleting glabrous twigs of
pedunculate oak, is the old gold fret
of the waning early March sun, and
the rising white of the full worm
moon. And in the last of the light, in
the woodland just in front of us, a
heart attack of a crack and Fin barks,
someone is shooting the crows.

Threaded with the months to be

(a north easterly, beneath Fin's pee tree)

A jive of a jackdaw morning. There is almond blossom pinking sinking and smattering the white. In the withering wild weft following blizzard sown snow blown in slantwise horizontal to the ground, there is a vertical diving and wheeling in squadron formation, a banking sharply and upending, then a clap flap-scattering before vast chattering then a settling and a perching in pairs. Jackdaws are filling bronchial branches, bracing ruffling, and remaining unflung. And suddenly silent and almost still, they are articulating leaves in the spare nearly bare budding early March trees. The pissabed yellow mimosa in full fluffy flower is heaven-scenting. Fin and I are freezing.

Ides of March – dropped blue

(the body formed in the female in which the development of another takes place; I'll never believe that the first egg burst before its mother was out of her shell)

It was an egg. It was broken. Apostatic and unwoken. Green-blue and heavy freckled, fractured from falling. Low in a witch-hazel, a wattle of twigs, a plaster of mud, a lining of grass. Wet weft and derelict. Fin dripping is square-pointing. There are four more dropped blue, a clutch stopped, inviolate and ides cold. It is still drizzling, and in a scant mist that is rising, the slight sharp sherbet scent of marzipan, frangipane, vixen and yolk yellow pollen frost.

the breaking of buds

(a circadian performance, after chilling time & short days)

It was young buds. Just starting from
the line of life, phloem sap climbing,
a shoot apical meristem and post
zygotic. It was bud-set and after an
accumulation of February's chilling, it
was scale leaf elongation, and then it
was a *Castanea sativa* bud breaking.

Vernalised, it was plum-purple and
very small. Yesterday basally-green it
was protruding and hardly there at all,
and then today there was a synchrony
of rhythms among the different
tissues and a saw-toothed leaf was
suddenly arisen.

It was the movement of an opening
following the termination of a closing,
it was perfect precision and the first
foliar flush. There was a celerity of cell
expansion and the emergence of
green. It was lanceolate formation
and from the source to the sink, it was
hormonal. It was transcriptional
signalling and the oscillating
patterning of the expression of Spring.

It was easy to split, hard to bend
sweet chestnut stems & a sheltering
from the wind. It was the longer days.

It was the weather staying mild with intermittent spit, mizzle and slight wild again. And growing slowly glossy green, it was again, circadian.

Imprimatur – felt & mould, ditching
(let it be printed, the land never forgets)

It was the tilth of the field, open to
loss and the crows' ghosts flung over.
It was the stubborn grass and the
ditches, trickling. It was the wild garlic
under the stricken ash, it was the oak
and the splash. It was the Stour
swollen. And from up here on the
sown edge of the light-land fields of
scaldy sands, I saw barleybirds sky
larking in the green slight-spiking
through brown rib-rolled. And in the
lingering light I saw pricked out dark
circles scant rising, and in a scattering
of struck flint a clustering of fourteen
single rings, and in the dusk-bronze
shadows ditching, ploughed over and
out, crop marking.

In the time of muck spreading, *aspergy* springs up
(somewhere between the blue and the green)

This morning contrails cut the sky like a fence dividing the land. The rain tastes of sharp flint and ploughed fields. Thin sprue of new sparrow grass is green-sprung. The daffodils are declined.

Fin is scent overloading, and the bullocks are blowing. There is a steady substrate clanking from the tillage. A rear vertical beater and a terragator spreader are rhythmically spraying shit, a heartbeat of sorts. With each gear change Fin whale-eyed nose furrowed, snorts and sniffs wildly the whey white-stinking sky.

Melissomelos, green after the rain

As of all states the Monarchie is best,
So of all Monarchies that Feminine,
Of famous Amazons excels the rest,
That on this earthie Sphaere haue
euer   bin,
Whose little hearts in weaker sex
(so   great   a   field)
No powers of the mightest Males
can make to yield: They liuing aye,
most   sober   and   most   chaste,
Their paine-got goods in pleasure
scorne to waste.

It was a weave of bees, the heavy
sound of them, the pelt-brown of
them, the deep of them knit close in
the bole of the linden after the rain.
It was the scent of propolis and lime,
it was the green, and in the bent grass
and softness of moss, it was the
incoming surf of sunlight and the
warm swarm swaying scintillating
chromatically from B minor to just
below C5.

Astride the purple bruise of the
distance and in the spent weft of
blown lilac, sweet wormwood, and
wax, it was sixty-thousand hearts
floating in haemolymph and
sorrowing in D   whilst the downpour
disarrayed May.

In a low tone, talking to the sibilant
grass in consonant intervals, a lone
bombelyn is carousing a day's eye.

At the edge of April

It was the sea; it was prussian and grew
crab-apple green swept a weft in the April
wind raked flat back prone and velvet
sheening in the wet light; it was the
storey under the oaks soaked pitched and
toned sky scratching & the sun rose
murkily and low swells nippled the sea
bluely and then purpling to bruised sour
lemon in the thin wind swelling as the
wych elms spiked our faces as we walked
rinsed and counting frogspawn into
sheltered cold black pools well-watered
and the old sun catching black and
bedazzled bones of soaked oak skeft with
silver slivered light damp fern fronds still
tight, the smell of salt, green garlic tang of
ash and with our backs to the sea, we saw
blue bells curling.

In the midst of arsenic and tin / ~~April *disrumpere*~~ reverdie
(at the juncture of a repeating, sumer is icumen in)

The morning was gradually decaying, lead-tin and orpiment. And there was thunder. The wind came and went. The oak and ash were neck and neck, and in the harrowed light, I saw it was broken. It was disrelated, fey woven roots dislocated / ridge-split from shifted soil, deteriorated, and cut out from under. And on the rising of leaf, it was falling. It was still roaring in my ears, the river. Roiled over. All that talking water.

A cranic of ordinaries

It was an opiate evening. Things leaped a little, and ordinaries were strange. It was just after dusk, the earth was black and close, it was wonderful numb & smothery rich with sift and the smell of the warming soil. It was the width of the wald and its deep-ploughed parallels. It was the widened still and the spate of sweeping barley wingspread in the wantoning wind. And it was an alizarin sun growing madder. It was droop-hinged the cranic carrion crow bough-groaning her brood as silencing the bells she peculiared the blue.

Bluebell glue

(William Turner's Herbal 1568 – *The boyes in Northumberlande scrape the roote of the herbe and glew theyr arrows and bokes with that slyme that they scrape of*)

It was a muck spread of a morning. In vast clattering the jackdaws vertiginously dived. Fin ducked. Copper beech leaves rattled, oak leaves clung curled and in a sliver of slim sun, cast thin shadows. Creased clouds skimmed and in the weave from seed to flower, roots to tower, a soon to be horse chestnut poked amongst the aconites. Birch brash clashed and a blackbird flushed. And in the dew, there was writelinge and a welling up. And in the spikes of green, soon to be blue, and on the twigs of sticky buds, soon to be maroon, was a slyme clinching fastness glewing us to home as anciently as does minerality to bone.

Saturation point / a brief description of *caelulum* / springing
(sog, sodden, sod, fields filled full, turf, Isatis tinctoria, wet earth, the sagging of gods own country)

Porphyry was the morning. Lambent the sun and above, the sky was upside down. It was lucent, and almost green. Viridian and full of sæp. There was a pigeon wing crack, and the sky was unattached. The sound of blau and soil soaking. Valley fog was rising fast and there was a general lack. Fin and I were standing holding our ground. The fields were creaking, we were becalmed and in the still, the deep blue barley was pearled. In the orographic uplifting, every blade was beading. Keel-clearing, it was a slow beginning. It was a shifting, a steeping, and an aniline dissipation. And in the dripping, it was indigo.

All souls & blood feathers
(we are but decaying, let's go a-Maying)

It was a mettlesome morning, dishevelled with ancientry. The bombelyn were hiving and familiar fields were fey-woven & disarranging. There were sticky drifts wet-petalling the stubbles, and it was delicate with little greens and lyric. Alive with pretty flies a pile of blood-feathers in the margin mantled with mounds of purpling dead nettles and gizzard strandlings of string-thin entrailings, were droning in metallic azurite blue. It was May decaying.

A little after the seeds were sown

there was a liminal line. And now it was fraying. It was a shot bow, the first foliar flush glancing fastening hedgerows emerald and winter corn green. On the cusp, with the crisp crescent moon, of growing.

It was dawn and the larks were skying.

The containing of remains, or digging a whole

("Expulsion from Eden grows indistinct [...] with no disrespect to Genesis, Paradise remains")

It was the mud. Fin was digging it and I was putting it back. It was May and the soil was wet-sticky and black. In the hole and out of it, the soil was whole. There was a unity and no lack. In the hole was soil. It was a comprehensive various entirety; it was a universe of relatings. It was grown wild with worms and stones, and little bits of bones, moth wings, shells, togethering with weatherings, roots, mycorrhizal chatterings. Hallowed it was. Sand ground from fractured rock. It was the breaking of that and in the cracks, green was brown and in the growing there was frost and featherings and very soon a change set in and a river flew through and in the flowing, silt, and a place for paddling. There was a muddy bottom and shoals and banks and in the slow sediment, seeds and green were grown and, in the decay, *M. vaccae* and humus and in the mud, there were flats and a soft bed. And it was brackish, it was friable, it was the bottom of the sea and then it was the dwelling place of darkling beetles, rabbits, vixens and cubs, moles, snails and carapaced creatures. It was a

harmonious production presently
interrupted, and it was one grain
away from being the whole of the
world; a paradise of remains, barely
contained.

Before the canopy closes, ~~six feet a century~~

(H. non-scripta & Anemonoides nemorosa)

Unlettered, anciently and under-
storeyed, the wood bell violently
blues and thrusts green, spearing
inflorescence through humus,
exhuming ~~history~~ scarlet elf cups.
Which bloom. Under the shadow of
alder, burnt umber and bone black, a
rhizomatous continuity of saprophytic
fungi and slow wood anemone.

Saxifrage

(Saxifraga granulate, or the ploughing of meadows in the midst of May)

the field is paused
enjambed

at every furrow
versed

and upon
each return

a red tractor

strode over by
an empty white sky

To come forth from an egg, altricial
(naked, blind, helpless)

And to fall or be pushed. A hatchling,
a fugitive scrap disbudded a catch in
the throat, skin silk-thin wet wrinkling
stitched red-capillaried stretched to
transparency, gape lead-tin yellow-
sticky wax-lemon flange-cornered
white-spike egg-tooth bump extruded
heart purpling there and here apteria,
a feather tract and natal down, a ring
of tiny bones blind eyed never saw
barely formed limpid and in the dew
and the long wet grass, neck sidled it
was raw, cold bluish grey davit and
dead.

Tortrix viridana, **silk ligatures and the incurling of leaves**
(the allofeeding of hatchlings and fledglings, squirm full of lime green caterpillar grubs)

It was a thin day. The sky was nameless and fading achromatically. All was unreliable. Except for the oak, which was ancient. And in its first foliar flush full of the gathered bodies of birds, it was brim with oak leaf rollers rapping sap with the sound of rain on the tremulous bones of its wavering host. Leaves ligatured were tight curled inward. And skeins of green were ravelling, dangles of lime wriggling, and from pulled silk stranglings, passerines were billfull of squirms. And above all that violence, a slow-spreading thread of crows rose over the indifference of bluebells, inclined in decline.

Birching; with two small wings & casting no deep shadow, a birch pioneers

(edge razor-strop fungus & witches' broom composed with Betula pendula)

It was a fair evening, in a subliminal kind of way. The sky was wearing thin. Of weather, fine and dry, the wind was south easting. My ears were wassailed by the sounds of small wings and my hair was full of bat. There was half a moon, barely that, above the filigree-ash slightly lit. There was otherwise slant-wise indifference and a light shiver through the stippling birch as lime-white curls unfurling verso slowly shed stripped-back bark revealing shadow-less a brittle-heart laced with witches' gall and riven with *Piptoporus betulinus*.

Found, gardening the old grounds
of a TB Sanatorium at the end of May

It was an odd bone, wizen. It cast a
shadow of absence; it threw me. In
the fennel and the scent of that, and
the caraway and angelica, in the
sappy lime and acid yellow of that, a
bone on its own, in the soil, troubling
the green. A grave, an ark, one inside
the other, and beside me the green
house a glass sky and inside gravely
in deep dark pots the seeds, still as a
soul, slow starting to green and grow.

Tyndall scattering;
the shimmering of tillering barley at dusk
(newly emerged lustre of Patania ruralis)

It felt like ancientry. The swallows
around my knees, hurtling. And clouds
of little brown moths, all the colours
of dusk and fallow, and the crows
rising slowly over

and in the waves returning navy
through the choppy sea of blustering
barley, there were no boats bobbing
in the tillering green and no foaming
white horses

there were squintings and slantings of
low gold sunlight, and thin in the
shadows between, a glancing vixen
padding. And, as she brushed
brambles at the fields edge, she sent
shoals of mothers of pearl winging in
a glimmering swimming-sky scattering
over the settling barley a
pruinescence of scales and the copper
glitter of diffracting motes of moth
dust, colloidally suspended in gold.

the silence of nests, left

On days like these, a pair of dead wren fledglings, the unbearable perfume of June, and sap rising. It was a gap in the air, the birds that weren't there. It was dawn, just past dark. The silence was stark and then the fat hatching moon cast off, snatched strawberry shadows in the oak and around my knees, the swallows pitch and yaw. It was a moth of a mourning and then low slow canto contralto; a cuckoo was calling.

Feeding on oak

(on the cusp of dusk on the longest day, and counting)

Fin and I and all those gaps in the sky
of all the moths that don't fly to
light and all those bone fires now ash
and reverting roses dropping slight
pearl petals caught in tortrix tight silk
swinging much as trout on taut wire
and the cuckoo calls and repeats and
I, I am counting, and she the tawny
owl responds, and we, we are falling
down the night.

The workings of willow; beaten from sallow saplings

(The Dingy Shears)

This is laden land, gospelling goat willow and moth-beholden. Fin and I, wayside, luring lunar-spotted partials to honeydew in the half-light, saw you. Squatting in the sallow, we were lurking there where the willow withies. In the quaking grass roots watching you drawing together the terminal leaves of a shoot hard by our sugar patch and there on the wetter darker hidden parts and wet-twisted worked out of stumps spiked with wassailings of new straight-shooting stems, were your rufous-suffused brood of caterpillaring *Fissipunctia ypsillon.*

In the smalt twilight of a stranded moon, a lime hawkmoth is faltering
(Mimas tiliae)

It was a simmer dim of a dusk, a fleet-bleat before midnight, the silver birch and small-leaved limes were glittering, and the leading-edge shadow of the scant smalt moon was stranded crystalline in rahj al ghar. Fin was exhuming his bone. And in the gloam, forewing tattered, a fading *tiliae* hawkmoth came scalloping unsteadily to light.

The entrapping of spikelets

(conversion of random oscillation into directed motion, the spiking of Fin)

Today is a day for prolonging the blue. The grass is bleached sharp white, and foxtail barbs bite, snaring Fin. The sky has stopped. The light is polished marble, the softest rock, tilting this hard land. Today is a day for ratcheting, for sticking and catching, today is a day for the stealing of motion, for friction, for spindling. And then for burying.

Learning to feed in the dark

(artificial light at night adversely affects the learning and motor control of young moths)

It wasn't a three-dimensionally printed artificial flower fitted with a motion sensor in its nectary. And it wasn't discarded after computation of flower interaction time and found flailing.

It was a nocturnally-scenting honeysuckle flung over the arcing luminescence of an old gold rose. And it was a young moth, a flower-naïve crepuscular hawkmoth seeking sugar.

It was overcast, there was no moon, just a little low light. It was locked on parallel processing, its feathered antennae ranging. It was upending inflorescence and flickering back, it was looking for nectary openings and dipping for geometrical clues.

And flower-tracking, with repeated return hackings, it was learning to feed in the dark.

~~Nearly as tall as me~~; shrinking

(Micromys minutus)

It was a susurrating meadow of a morning, micro-lepidoptera rose flickering jerkily in clouds above tribes as we parted an acre of ox-eye daisies, wild carrot, cornflowers, poppies, campion, fox tail, mallow, coltsfoot, ragwort, tansy, wild bergamot and thyme, honeysuckle, hazelnut, bramble, Scots thistle, red fescue, and curling vetch nearly all as tall as I. Parting the way through, Fin finds her by a deer-stomped patch, balled in a tall tight weave of desiccating thatch, smaller than my clenched fist, as high as my waist, the spherical house of a single harvest mouse.

I have two meadow brown butterflies in my hair. Fin is clung with cleavers and a scatter of seeds and on my knees, I was talking to a solitary bee circling stigma, and we were all shrinking.

Fin and I, we were filling the gaps unpinning the moths and on days like these we were only ever nearly as tall as all of the tribes on this slight ball of spun & spider full grass.

It was a morning for thinking small,
for filling the cracks. For inspecting
bracts for angels enclosed in glumes,
and for other hoverings about
awnings and lodicules, and for
spiralling proliferous. And for tiny
diptera in the *Cynosurus,* and for the
Southern hawker. And above us,
umbrels of wild carrot keeled in poa,
the shadow of a red kite turning
around a cuckoo calling, and out of
the indigo a fall-streak hole is
punching open the sky.

The growing of glass: in the TB San pit

(knapped flint cracked shines and fractures just like glass, the bled out of the decomm'd Sanatorium still capillary rising)

It was a hindering. This place in full-sight, well-hidden. The ritual of that, the myth. The order that isn't. It was a claiming moon, proclaiming hay harvest and the calm of that. It was a staying place. A pit of glass, part grown over, part caved in. The tang of tin and bluebottles, ampoules-unstopped blet perfume warrened-out by rabbits, burrowed-bone unsettlings in bedsprings, copper wire, handle less pans and mangles. Tuberculosis cures that didn't. Above, spindles and hazelnut, medlar and dog rose. Marbles adrift, bent spoons. Meadow browns. In the mix of glass, I feel stone. And the slips in the gaps. The red shift. The primeval shadow. The lack. *Requiescat.* Shallow shucked remains of a burial woven with roots, and in the Spring, with shoots. Negotiating broken. *In pacem.* Revenant. And in melanic form, Dark Arches and sweet chestnut with silica strewn by Fin, bits of battered tong and blade buried by change, unearthed in fun; rabbits scattering over the emptiness of old glass, pot boilers and flake-sharp flints of resinous grey. A flindering.

We follow the fox this way every day and, in the rain we see the glinting arisen growing again, fractures moving upwards through the soil. Hagridden, I collect the decades for fear of Fin's paws.

Full tilt; double-ended worlds

(the tropic synchronicity of root and shoot in July)

This was a morning for moving in both directions at once. Not moving backwards then forwards, not one at a time. And not being stretched which is no real growth just a thinning and a soon-to-be breaking and a rapid diminishing as Fin shows me when we tilt a bit and comes apart a drowned coney kit I wish he hadn't found. This all-at-once, this is both the growing downwards and the growing upwards, a thickening and a strengthening. It is a going of both ways oppositely and a going of the same way simultane. Roots down head up, a double-ended world. What we do is what we can in synchronic equilibrium.

After the divorce

(participating with cinnabar moths)

Chthonic was the dawn. It was
inscrutably blue. I was trying not to be
a keystone species, not to reside in
the place where Plato and Persia
collide. It was a quarrel of a morning
between priests and kings. It was a
diminishment and despite the
dragonflies hawking in the canopy of
oak, I was trying not to be

but the morning was stalled. Then we
found a flattened place of dead
shreds & new white bones, and in the
slanting bleach of desiccating foxtail,
there were cinnabar moths and an
old pond

crazed with gnats and brittle, then
through a fold of Suffolk sheep and a
gathering pen, we reached the
middle ground, and found it was a
freed field of just cut wheat, risen
with nodes of flint, goatsbeard ghosts
and spiralling, it was eleusinian.

Nocturning

("Angels (it's said) often don't know whether they're moving among the living or the dead." Rilke, The First Elegy)

but nature exhausted by the turning
of night away, still. Hushed. And from
the silence of the fugitive dark, the
ness of dawn taking slight a pale
shape a thin promontory reaching
into the spittle of land pricking out
here thisness and that first slant
alighting on purpling flowerheads
erupting a capitulum of crowns and
picking out myriad gaps of absence
around ghosts of Thistle Ermine and
Antlers, Bells, Brocades and Quakers.
The loss of all those angels watching
for the hour of turning, lamenting the
extinction of instance and precipitous
decline.

The impairment of adhesion & the uniformity of it all

(the structure of resistance, the threshing of husks)

barley bent heads wet with summer showers smell like young yeast and grain. Malt over twenty acres of filled folded ears not a single swallow, no swifts, no larks, no clouds of flies, no crows, not a single tortoiseshell, no peacock butterflies and no crowds of meadow browns, no crepitation, no stridulating, and no standing proud of adhered husk and caryopsis in a stiff straw sea

we saw an efficiency of sky becalmed and conservative consistency, we saw uniformity of grain and stasis, and the maintenance of the same. Fin and I, wrist and knee skinned slipping in the rain, are tumbling between parallel lines of silent grain and between this and that ethylene phenotype and this and that nud-like pericarp, we see the standing stillness of no differences at all.

In a field of just cut barley, rows upon rows of crows

In the just cut stalks of threshed stark
stalk, in the stubble rows, barley birds
aren't larks, they are crows.

The finding of blue

(how a feather falls, the tessellating light scattering reflective beads of camouflaged birds)

The evening was deliquescing, one
smudge at a time. All was drooping,
and the oaks were full of gall. Fin and
I were looking up through back-lit
flickerings watching a bickering of
concatenating jays high in the canopy
when we saw a single feather fall.
Dropping a fletch to the dripline edge
then reaching terminal velocity
drifting a little then down to the
ground where we found, surrounded
by brown, Monet's cerulean blue.

Depth of Field, The convergence of evolution; the dying of an eye

(Squirrel Study Reveals a New Path for Light Through the Eye – the bridging of compound eyes in arthropods with the camera eyes of vertebrates, – it was a mutual meeting on that bridge, right between our eyes)

Malachite was the morning; mallow was the rain. The clouds were mauve with indigo in a pigeon plumage kind of way. Fin and I, on cracked tarmac stopped between ditch and wire and on the puddling ground a dishevelled pelt was splayed. Soft and warm and velvet, foetal-curled and quiet, we saw a slight heave leave with a shallowing of breath, and then in the stretching instant of a syntax of sympathy I saw we in every cone of the aperture depth of the waiting to die obsidian eye of another mammal just as warm-blooded as me. It was the insistence of sentience in the recognition of kin. It was a rift of an encountering, and then the sun came out again.

Plump after feeding

(the learning of the killing skill)

It was an iron-bright of a morning. A
wake of buzzards was soaring, and
the valley was moving with fleering
rain through a pewtering sky of
stiffkey blue. A young dark morph of
a buzzard practising his killing skill
caught Fin's eye and beneath the
mewling eyrie pine we found their
charnel-spattered ground. It was an
after-the-rain after-the-plough bird
strike of a precisioning and then a
sudden disarticulation as the buzzard
fissured the kit and then flensing it
left it for dead with the same fast-
thin slit gamekeepers make between
sinew and bone in the hind of a
ferret-won doe, threading one dead
leg through the other crosslegging a
truss then all lain out in a row. These
long days blow like wild roses in the
rain.

Fin & I on a ride in a dark wood
in a sudden summoning of summer thunder squall

In the blister-song of witness, call-me-raw-claw ochre red kite highly gyringling sipping from the clouds' frost crystals. Sister-me Southern Hawker glisteningly slipping between skimmers of wet nettle leaves skidding droplets showering me stunningly. Wonder me Fin square-pointing me the oak wound roundedly with tighteningly twistingly ivy-clouding us with Mothers of Pearl swimmingly shivering just barely-beingly there. Standing me up staringly making me fly, Fin hound-of-more-than-brother me singingly wingedly as we are both flung takeningly rambustingly slantingly brightly through water rushing gustingly dashingly dark lashingly riddening tawnies joining us on our owling ride of a slide of wet earth stone flingingly entanglingly flightily vanishingly right up to the sky

A dog fight

(moths, moons & mushrooms; the flaunting of speed and the dying of dragons flying with bats at dusk)

It was an imbrication of a dusk, one for walking with trees. Moths were coming with us like the mountains don't, along with ocra rossa-tinted bees, a meadowfull of crepitating crickets and Odonata darting. Casting for the sturgeon supermoon it was the pipistrelle bats which saw to the fall of the hawkers, and the divestment of spitfiring wings. It was ancestral, the flexing and the twisting, the variable curvature and the avoidance of stall. It was motion-camouflage and the emergence of wrinkles on anciening wings, and in the stark backlit moon light it was a skimmering, a clasping, a sprawling and a dashing. It was a dog fight. Under the noctule roost, through the luna-stricken oak, a bright-lit shimmer of a stilled pile of air-filled wings, severed. Fin, nosing oak leaves and fat full moons of puff balls ground growing, shows me. Dropping, he rolls. He loves the blet scent of dead.

Dog days, rain after *dies caniculares*
(land scrapings)

It was a drift and a grain of a morning, and in the rift the spilling river was running spate-fast indenting and undermining, flensing and silting its bendings. In wet wheat slanting, Fin and me standing at the valley head scouring, we saw the land move – its slaking scree sliding sift-slow reposing hollowing down the fall, and we ankle-deep were in the morning of the night before. It was a rinsing flickering of sharp-shingling grit, a chopping constellating shifting and heliacal, it was an exhumation and a germinal rising.

And then a breaching, a ferment, and a tilting at disseverings, a swelling of the soil, and in the upwelling the sun unearthed was vermilion. The land was returning, stranging runnels filleting and gullying, and in the disinterring Fin had found bone, a rib and then a skull. Fox-dishevellings.

Hovering *as it were fallen angelles*
(composition after arising)

In the space between wings, a
dementing of dragonflies, a wind
hinged and a displacing and replacing
of the trace of a hawkmoth hazarding
a flickering in the wheat-heat of a
dusk soon to be dark, in that place to
taste the scent of hyphaloma rising,
blackberry must and honey-suckling.

In the flowering of moths after
pupation soft bodies bewildering up
into the night, before the declaiming
of conifers under a hung sun emptied
of all but blet scent sent to fetch you,
before   encountering,   before
nectaring, before enrapturing, before
the thistle down capturing you,
before the beginning of me seeing
you   there,   then   seeing   you
everywhere, before the opalescent
rising of Mothers of Pearl thrown up
like spoiled negatives smudged &
slight spiralling to light, in the space
before all of that bright exposure,
the long wait, the suspension and
stilliche of a myrios of lost moth
hoverings.

Marcescent was the morning, sublimen the scent of death

(elements of decomposition, ripe over the edge of autumn)

It was a tenderer dirt, loam after rain soft and tractable, the uplands were stubbles of corn, the scent was a common glory. The air was faint with it and Fin sudden was in full pelt across the shawm stalks like a vast scramble of blown leaves in the old summons of a summer storm. The sky was narrow and mantling. There was a cloistral gleam, the edges were breathing green, and over watching Fin, a haunting of rooks were harrowing. In the deeps of fingerling shadows below the stag's head oak a hollow of crazed hound grass and a young fallow deer, car up ended, mazed with maggots and flies was fraught and blawan. Fin was ancestoring. Rolling he was bringing that scent-trove home.

The detachment of distance, as the crow flies

(the way home is far and not far)

Schists and lodes flint the spark. The
rain off-kilters ghost ponds and Fin,
an island, stands wrist raised blood
mixing with silt and swelling taint-
ditching. We hobble the ridge, the
storm subsiding as the soil trails grit
through sand and in the rivulets, I
wash his flint-torn paw. Sun streams
vivid green and I pack wet bracken in
my shredded sleeve and bind Fin and
then fletching the low hung horizon
for the nearest line to a place, detach
a slant-flight distance in furrow-flung
geometry, and we follow stone-slow
the long scant shadow making for
home.

Greenish

(the curdle of weft light of the second august supermoon)

The moon looms. We weave
haphazardly between thistle fluff
tufted raggedly by glancing
goldfinches. In a curdling milk-stout
light, two stoats are erraticing, and
Fin is entranced by their frantic
weaving. Every ligament taut, skin
rippling Fin waits sparking, his ears
quivering and the young rabbit, stoat-
dazed stopping dead in its tracks ears
flat back crouches down stone still
eyes obsidian waiting for the kill. Red
thread pulled. It is fast
dispatched. The light is greenish, and
the whey moon is blue.

They don't eat the wings

(a prey comes apart, a short history of de/coupling)

Feather follicles of the wren in the
sedge sense feather-motion, vortex-
growth and shedding. And the wings
of the Yellow Belle powering up just
below are populated with airflow and
strain sensors capturing point
measurements as buckling its wings it
elides the slight watching wren. The
dragonfly's directional gaze follows
reflexive saccade then in a smooth
pursuit-movement,   takes off
predicting when the Yellow Belle will
cross the azimuth. The wren watching
again side-eyes the dragonfly, young
and shining, just emerged. The moth
flickers. Two robins unconstrained by
prey motion statistics, intercept the
morning and striking a yaw and roll,
they pitch fast and terminate the
dragon's flying.

Mutinus caninus

(dog stinkhorn, sticky spores and detritivores)

It was a seeping rotting meat of a mycelium morning. Fin was pawing the deadwood boggy ground, and the scent was *impudicus* and high. In a scuttle under brush, September elder stained and purpling, there was inflection, a moving around, an echo of the land. And in a dancing of dizzying diptera, a brash clamour and a simmering, a keeling stipe henge of glebous sticky tips was spore-laden and making mast. Madder-root pink topplings of honeycombed rings of witches fingers were bright & stinking

Taxonomy of a view, rising to the top
(particle sorting, granular convection)

Ash (hollow trunk, filigree) and acorns, autumn (starting), apples (fallen), aspen (white);

Blackbird, blackberry, bindweed, bird cherry (wild), birch (silver), beech (dead), brambles (twining), a blackcap, bluetits and wild carder bees;

Chickens, convolvulus, carrot (wild), cabbage white butterfly (large), coltsfoot, cherry (bird), chestnut (sweet), conkers (lime encased and spiney), crickets stridulating & dark clouds;

Dogs (two, hearts of mine), dragonflies (turquoise, blue and hawking), darkling beetles on dead wood;

Echinacea (growing wild), elderberries (black and falling);

Fallen feather (white, near-fungi), fox scat and foxtails (waving);

Ground (rising), greengage trees, grass of every shade of green (going to seed and bleaching), gold leaves (inward-rolling) and gall wasps, grasshoppers (crepitating) and gold finches (tussling with thistle fluff);

Hazel, honeysuckle, hornets (three), hillocks of hound grass, helicoptering sycamore seeds, hedgerows (overgrowing, full of hips & haws);

I & a hive of huge old ivy filling an old low oak, skirts to the ground (mice-skittering), the beginning of in (here);

Jet-black sloes, jet-black jackdaws, jewelled wings of crows;

Kites (thermaling, fox-red and calling);

Light, little-leaved limes, leaves falling, lilac (green), a lizard (on a log eye-to-eye with a dragonfly);

Medlar, mulberry, mulch, mushrooms, moss, maples (leaves turning), meadow browns (seven), moths (day-flying), magpies (shouting), a muntjac (barking) and mallow flowers (mauve & purpling);

Nightshade (deadly), nettles (tall and wince-stinging);

Oaks (ancient and stag-headed), oats (wild and desiccating), orchard (bat-filled and laden);

Plants, pear trees, pears (hard), poa, plums, poppy pepper-pots, pond plus life;

Quince (fruit-burdened);

Roses (wild, red-hipped and shiny), rumex (sheep's), robin (red), red admiral (nectaring on a plum, deep purple, German) and a rabbit (young, sitting & dying, myxied);

Strawberries (wild), seedheads (acres), sunflowers (corn), senescence starting, squirrels (grey), shadows (lengthening), soil (dry) and a stag's head (supplanted by a crow);

Trees, trees, trees, teasels and thistle fluff and a tawny owl (male, calling, much too early);

Under-storey (shaded, silent);

Vetch (purple, wild), vipers bugloss (heavy with tired, sunbleached & pollen-dusted bees);

Walnut trees (two), water (wondrous, dark, toad and weed-filled), wasps, wrens (darting), a woodpecker (shrill & green) and wood pigeons (billing & courting, slap-clapping and falling);

Xenos (the space between the space between the space between leaves, the state of being a guest, a host, a stranger);

Yellow yellow yellow, sunflowers (corn), yarrow (white); and

Zinc (corrugated, bright in the sunlight-lidding hot compost heaps, decaying).

We crows know. We know.

(Corvus corone, everything does what it needs except the human which does what it wants)

This is the rattle of the corn, this spent sift of a morning striding into creaking stubbles, flitching in the white dawn, a chorus of sorts. This is corn, stiff, cut down in rows, unbending, small stalking susurrating crow full, spun silk full, wide September sky full, stilted.

These crows gutturally utter clamour and in uncertainty flex applications of statistical inference based on experience. Syllabic and sibilant they canticle each row, sassing through short grasses. Blown backwards. Claw full. Corded. Let there be unruly syntax, and cranics of carrion crows. Waiting for it to happen. The way it happens. Knowing.

The disturbing of owls

(Latin rudere "to roar, bellow," Old English reotan "to be/wail, lament.")

The owls are howling out the dawn, whisperings of charcoal creep as the moon withdrawing slight-purples sloping under-edging with short-shadows bluing. Forlorning, the tawnies are calling back and forth. This morning, they are resounding out of place. Ruderal, this wood thick with the whining of chainsaws and dull thuds.

Ruderals, the seeding of weeds
(elaiosomes, the sowing of wild oats, rubble grown)

Wild relatives of these close-shorn &
static fields of wheat, barley, and oats
once   vagabonded   over   vast
disturbances of fracturing continents,
far-drifting & allocating patterns of
genotype matching lands travelled,
and in compatibility making seeds
variably adapted for short and long
haul flights and for short and long
dormancies, waiting out eons of
unpredictable   disturbances   &
variable nights, niche-breadth held,
yielding little save survival diversities,
rich in lipids and dispersed by ants.

Warped in the upright loom – spindling

(giving pink to the sky)

In thin thrumming with slight high
whining of striped hover flies a
canticle of hum, a/ euphonic
insertion, a tender of yarn strong-
threaded the spindle of berries burnt
orange, edge-weft fields linnet-pink
& vatic.

On our knees, pleurant for the deceasing of bees

(only bees can fertilise selfheal by landing on its lower petal lip and nectaring for honey at the base of the corolla tube. The hooklike corolla was said to heal wounds incurred from the lookalike sickle & scythe mowing of meadows. Selfheal creeps low in curled purple through flailed grasslands.)

It was a smoulder of a dusk & around the edges mist was damp. The moon-rising was on the cusp of going over. In September wasps sting hard and towering nettles in full seed raise cystolithic weals. Exhausted bees, pollen-clotted in defeat cross over membrane-thin abraded wing tips, clutching swaying Self-heal clasped gisant. Fin is scenting the air, dying honey and the declension of small-leaved limes arising. Gentling herbaceous, the meadow-creeping purple-blue is slow-declining. There is a risk of rain & the moths are frayed

The unravelling of littoral

(this is not a flat place, this is a limicole morning, at the margin of the day)

Polder-warped the shallows, scapula, shoulder blade skelf shelf shovelled. This land sounds of ocean, wind through wheat, ownerless sea of hard stalks and siltings. Levelled. This rut, that rote, rutter, plough-furrowed route descrying the curve of the horizon. This land, beyond that ocean of sibilant starlings gleaning stiff-threshed husk, is looked over. *This land is not flat.* This thread of the warp, this loaming, this scried vast selvage is overlooked land. Limicoline this land, this looming-indistinctly, this land a marge, and inalienably this land is sea.

Perpetual gravity – Box Tombs at Wiston

(the quality of appearing to recede, essential to the landscape tradition)

Now illegible, ~~the children of John Whitmore and Susanna his wife,~~
~~Sarah aged 11 Months,~~
~~Robert aged 2 Years,~~
~~Rebeckah aged 11 Months,~~
~~Elizabeth aged .... Weeks,~~
~~Lucy aged 1 Week,~~
~~Susanna aged 20 Years,~~
~~Thomas Aged 6 Years.~~
~~John Whitmore departed this life Jany the ....6th 1746 Aged (6)6. He was a good husband loving father faithful friend and a Good Christian. Susanna Whitmore died / Jany. 25 1789 Aged (?8)6.~~ To dwell until all the world inscribed when it was still possible to die. To lie slightly foxed, mortared in a brick box irregularly repaired, alive with stone-devouring lichen and littered with dry lime, leaves and frass. Fin pees antimony and sees off the squirrel, wards off unbelievers we have no need for having no place amongst toppling tombs. A litany indescribable, a conjugation beyond reach, an accent mark over a vowel, an entire landscape made grave. It was October, the same fields were ditched, furrowed, carved, still dug over and still the Stour was flowing. In

the picture's distant plain, the sun
like other yellows, was still fading.
Generally, a history remains unsure.

The listing of the sky, glazed with red madder

(Carrot from the Celtic is red of colour, and Daucus is from the Greek dais to burn; list is to lean or incline, to please, to desire, lust after, to listen, to try to hear, to pay attention, a border or borderlands and Chaucerian lists were places, like borders, of tournament or combat. From the sense of edgy border, comes order in rows, groups, strips and in always incomplete lists of things)

It was a raw-earth umber of a morning, one for standing still in wild carrot umbels spider-spun & lysting with tall dog-grass all hung-over. Coarse-toothed nettles were swaying, and long seed-bundles of frosted geometric clusters drooped. In the great green sea of crepitating sedge, Fin and I were tilting for any slighting on the edge of the zinc scent of the blustering wind, hoping again for hard rain, for inclination & for the ozone spray of white spume horses. Scant, the purpurin was fading. Streaked with streaming lake and madder, we were leaning into the whipping wind & hearkening. Fin and I, listing into the shudder & the soddening, the flattening & the dark, uproarious & outrunning the suddening and in the roiling roust about of lead-tin yellow, the sky inclined to one side, was sour swallowing the sun.

Home with missing trees; loss of lintel & transom

Vatic was the evening and the scents were rising. Fin was a flash of a nose grazing the ground following fey lines crisscrossing the lay of the land. I was following. And at the top of the hill, coalescence, and in the gap between oaks, an overcoming. The sky was pulling through, ultramarine and brimming. The clouds were thin spun white with kites scrimmaging, and below, forty-three cricket bat willows stumped. Thick with puddled mud, the snicket brash and sawn wide open. Down below, a felled ash, bone black with burning. Above still the kites are circling on thermals. To think I'm of an age that can see the change, all those trees from their beginning, the smell of raw honey and balsam and now all I'm seeing are prophecies but once I saw and having seen I remember everything.

Brown earth

(Argent was the sky, a ferric wildish light)

It was antique, the evening with light like grass collapsing in autumnal flare, and silvered thistledown wildish. The sky was curlicued with the scent of burning bone, and from a stand of sodden sheep, reaming steam was rising. Tilth was running off, torrenting and careering. In pendent fall maples leaving buttercup and vermillion were goldening to a wet conker-brown. Sliding down the valley long shadows of diving kites spinning through inhalation, fox a-racketing black chattering of dusking crows. Then in the stop & the still, the Stour mud heavy-dulled full of field & drowned, tugging lysting trees, overwhelms and inundates a vast deflation. The earth was green, madder the lake, iron-salted & oxalated, ferrous the ground now all washed over with a slow eddying of Van Dyke brown.

Other greens; a burst of lucidity & tenebris

(between the reflected sky and inundation, a scant difference in pitch; between greens, the shadows of spillings & erasings)

Whichever way Fin & I cut through you, you're green. Colour all the way through & in between. The woods flooded, water green and green earth brown all the way down and standing. The ground and trees drowned, twigs stitched to the sky leak deep green and ditches tip over land, erasing. Glauconite-shadowing layering malachite over imprimitura – fading, leaving verdigris alchemically-glazing Scheele's green, a *lucidis intervallic* kind of sea glass a drift with silts of copper & fallen leaf. A transparency, the growing sky a wash; the great green solved to a wet grass sweep of raking saturation.

Beyond leaf fall, the arrest of autumn, making islands of green

(the turning of senescent leaves back on again, the remaking of photosynthetic green)

Metronomic, neonates spreading on slivering silk threads weaving between the canopies of soon-to-be senescent trees, are rappelling down sunlit strands swung-weighted by luminous greens, a bright dialectic between burnt-umbrous and fulvous-fallow leaves.

Phytophagous caterpillars' oak-leaf mine cytokinin, making verdant chlorophyll islands in soon-to-be abscised leaves, stalling the fall.

Unfurling curling autumn, *lepidoptera* and *wolbachia* in synchrony are manipulating green & with the fresh foliar flush of a false imposter Spring, are making old leaves turn young again.

It was the Orionids, *Nov. 3, 2023, Suffolk, England*

(That I should have lived nearly fifty years without knowing him, shews too clearly what sort of observer I have been. [John Quincy Adams: Diaries 1779–1821, diary entry for Nov. 18, 1813, St. Petersburg, Russia])

It was a blanching fragile verglas night, the moon was a lump in my throat, a suprasternal tightening and canescent. Like plants grown to haulm under the cover of darkness, branching limbs were etiolating and bifurcating alveoli spreading skyward were reticulate. We, Fin & I, were watching the plough when a welding arc sudden-flared and in the glare of the streaking brights and showers of vaporous white, we saw cometary trains, long and fast, and in the silence and eburneous light we were stark, Fin & I, just standing there staring out into the revelating dark. It was radiating, constellating and meteoric, it was a gasp and a short sharp bark, it was the astronomic autumn shooting of the Orionids.

The woof of the woods; the predated spread of fallow bones

(weft threads running lengthwise against the December sun)

Fin & I, we visited the visitors of bones, the thread of the fabric of the floor of the woods across which the woof is thrown. The cast of the net of the long shadows of trees slant to up-flung trunks and the wry warp of rime. Fin spindles a wrangle and fettles a turn and there are vertebra versus a mal-version of ribs and half a set of hips. With a wrinkle and a wriggle Fin writhes a raphe and there's him rhapsodic, subverting the skull, odd-socketed, spread-and-wrest mandibular, *Dama dama* ungulate with rows of tooth well-verst.

Standing, not flying

(earth bound, like a fallen constellation, salting)

It was a kind of archaeology, a trajectory of mud, frozen over. The equivocal sky and an equinoctial moon, rising. The stars were articulating fractals in a frost-bound fog and the weight of that slew through stripped-back oaks, bare-standing inordinate & tall, blood-drawing. And there in low-looming the barn owl, bone-spiked kite, fret-working & letting me know unarguably that I wasn't made to fly.

Positively knowing Strigiform, phosphorescent pale-spread leading-edge myth-moth glowing & salting the dusk with mycological musk, and I, unquiet I, try my own feather-bereft scapula, seraphim stumps, unholy wings. Whilst you, pre-historic you, skim stubble, glitter fringing vestigial leaves releasing the smell of fungi and toads heavy with the coming snow.

In particularities; coming out of Kingsland Lane into an ordinary December day

(walking through a crept of wet wild thyme & a weft of sodden leaves)

Canaletto blue, the sky as direct as
that. Fin & I were jostling for space
with leaves and centuries of kings
trampling slick light into wet mud
on the eponymous land's lane. There
have been horses this way. And
archers. And angels. Thyme, crushed
apple and loam, the sour yellow
lichen and a winter moth's flight from
startling. These are ordinary trees in
ordinary rain in the ordinary mud of
an ordinary day in the bleaching way
of a low sun almost white, a split flint
on the line of the horizon. Fin & I
watch it flare and shift the earth
rinsing us with the ploughed-out
colours of mid-December and the
ripped scent of the raised ribs of the
old resettling ground.

Stickleback winter, having broken the surface

(in the prickle of slight rising winter wheat, sticklebacks stranded)

This is an old river with an old name, strong stirring and returning. After rain, uproar and convulsing through land that wet works stiff. Stanstickles bony process prickle backed glitter fill stetches and magpies clawfoot grub for squinny silverings, hopping detritus flooded hollows snatching biblical catch stanked in furrows. Dank sprickles tarnished rot as overtopping swims swale & nickled roky mud remains, twitch choked with barely wheat, glint flicker flaring plashed fire tracing, in drownings, the race of mare's tails above.

Rendering the oblique sensation of being as close as this

Ambiguous was the dusk, stippled cerulean sunk to glutinous blue then grey and hung somewhere between a thought and a feeling as the monopodial points of empty trees were flaring ember, blown to the moment of fire, impossible to paint the pivot of change and now the slight curve of a new moon and its orbiting star. This transcript Aristotelian, the air – bright catchcold and fractal, fret-shapes standing out on the horizon, a diminishing line disappearing, orthogonals receding, a settling of things. In the distance, an avoidance of the vanishing of points. What is missing and what remains. It is necessary to write what cannot be written. Mist is rising and in the parallels there is a suggestion of closer and of the deepening of a local spatial recession

Operophtera brumata (Linnaeus, 1758)
(*winter moths mating on cloudless mild nights*)

They aren't leaves, clung appurtenant to deep-trenched bark and bare low-hanging skirts, they are nubs crawling up from mud-buried pupae out from littered foothills of the old pollard oak, newly-budded. Almost apterous they are pheromone soaking & wafting, waiting on violence having just vestigial apologies for wings. There is glitter and flicker-dust, distance & embedding and in the mild calm night no diminishing of perspective. Only ordinary moth magic spiralling towards to the horns of the slow-rocking moon, hung dripping.

It was a green Christmas

Today is a morning for hoarding
the sky. The first day. There is a
struggle of sunlight and hips are
claw-raw crimson sprawled in the
crisp clasp of cold cerulean blue.
The jackdaws, old-scolding, are
storming a crow. Wry-rumped
bulging bees equipoised adhere to
spearing mahonia swagged in
hangs of lemon bright. Sour goslin
freaked with green quick the
queach and up pricks the fescue
and the twitches. This is witch soil,
and grass that grows in Janiveer is
grass that grows no more this year.
Today is already longer by a cock's
stride and the church yard is fatter.

How to see angels

("and each of them could show you a landscape as if for the first time")

The best way, of course, is to look. Like landscape, they are found inside, not outside. Like landscape, there is really nothing to be said about angels, or poetry. They always already own their own meaning. Words slide off. Aslant. They may not be described. They are. Thought full. There is no end to them. Every day they die. They are always already. And in their own blue shadow sunk.

Grazing light

(ploughing on Water Lane up on the ridge at the top of the valley, a red tractor gull-mobbed works up the rise and down, ploughshares on the turn glint, scratching the sky)

In the fissure-thick stilled viscosity of just-turned-brown ground, stopped & hung with sharp-angled gulls hurling upstrokes into the easterlies, the land too wet to plough, the surface defecting as the sky distorts its support. In the grazing light, craquelure and impasto, shallows & a raking rise of random strokes of gale fed rain following form and detachment, smooth and luminous against the grain, saints and other heroes slanted in contours under the intonaco crust of a glittering blood dusk run red pulling raw trenches deep six from flint drawn mud sliced in serried ranks of sulled incisions. Between the convolutions, drownings and scuddings of verdigris flare over uprootings, winking coin and the rot of what remains buried there.

Snow drops
(the way it was silent)

the way the echo across the valley took
seven seconds to stop, the way the
crows dropped, the way the snow fell
and is still, and is and is and is and is all

The way in which light falls
(the finding of form)

I am sending you hip red and azurite
blue and colours in between. The hard
hoar frost shot through with bright sun
light is sending every colour of the
rainbow across the fractalled crackling
icicled grass. There are colours
spattered every which way. Fin
absorbing them all in his sleek black
coat reflects back a violet purple, a kind
of velvet pansy wild and smoky fading
to rose madder then campion pink. On
finding form, light scatters. Fin's eyes
spark amber and flare. Whilst the
afternoons are growing longer, they
are still too short. The sun too molten
to watch dehisces slipping drip by drip
and we walk home cold in the fast-
dropped dark.

Mass
(the valley, disquieted)

Standing on long thin lignin shadows drawn slant of hedgerow oak. These fingerlings stretch rippled black over acres of plough-trenched earth. Parallel as waves, the soil a frozen ocean on the instant of the turning of the high tide. Sculptured, the furrowed field is hung immortalised on the in-breath between that scant moment and now. The land is still. The valley sketchy in breathy pink. The crows leaf the bare trees in silence. Only the sky moves.

the sky, stone. All the shadows gone.
Fin and I, standing on the ridge looking
down the valley. The mass prone, the
growing slow. This land is no place. This
land is time and in time this land will
bury us. Below, there's a mobbing of a
kite's vertiginous dive and sleek black
greyhooded jackdaws' carp and scuffle.

A toad-strangler of a day; usual a plash / In the plain

(*without struggle or fight, winter aconite*)

low down in the mud glossy petaloids
with unfused carpels, ranunculites with
sticky stamens of bright bitter Scythian
yellow glint gold in the half light, leaf-
like bracts cupping frost from which
emerge   unsteady   bees   struggling
heavy-legged   thrumming   and
overloaded with glycosidic toad venom

What blueness is this

(taking the air)

Broken glass arises with winter warrenings and decorates rabbits' scrapings where wild flowers grow. Powdered-penicillin ampoules make scatterings spiking mud nubbed with poison bottles blue as early bluebells poking through. Badgers strong-claw cures in the corner of this once-was tuberculosis sanatorium, showering soil-clung gobbets of serum vials, snapped glass necks, treading decades-old streptomycin into the celandines.

Transfiguration

(what looked like the edge being ploughed, turned out to be the horizon)

In this glutinous blue and ticky-tacky transcription of stifled light, it was an ordinary day and what wasn't blue, or oxide white, was green or ploughed brown with bone-black fenestration and a peppering of crows. And we could hear the buds breaking, the soil draining, and the silvering of the sky. It was an iridescent light, the form of the land hollowing and not a fence in sight. Walking, Fin & I, we never arrive. And the red tractor ploughs glittering lines through brown land, gulls following. We watch the brown umber to red ochre then smear to stiffkey blue. Owling, we smell torn soil and follow eye-marks of birds through violet mud sliding and uprising then we go over the edge carrying on bright over the horizon.

After words and some notes

Usual is wind from the east; the title is taken from the Celtic poem, 'Usual is the Wind' from the *Red Book of Hergest VI*. The mythological dog was Cerberus, companion of Hercules whose mother was Hecate, the goddess of witches, who had an affinity to blackthorn.

Scare crows, it was a blæc death, it was a murder; a group of crows is called a murder. When one crow dies, the murder gathers around. The funeral is not a mourning, it is a gathering to find out who killed the dead. The murder will then, en masse, mob the killer. I hope that happened here.

The closure of crocus; the epigraph in brackets references van Doorn and van Meeteren who are in turn referencing Pfeffer, 1873 and Andrews, 1929 in their Review Article in the *Journal of Experimental Botany* titled 'Flower Opening and Closure' Vol. 54, No. 389, pp 1801-1812, August, 2003.

Tread depth, earth gazing; the phrase in parenthesis paraphrases, with thanks, a line in Adrian Bell's article 'A Countryman's Notebook', first published in the *Eastern Daily Press,* 10th March, 1973.

Imprimatur – felt & mould, ditching; invisible, except in certain lights and at certain times of cropping, is an *Ancient Monument at Risk* in Wissington comprising fourteen Bronze Age ring ditches known as the Wissington Ring Ditch Cluster. It is generally to be found under approximately ten inches of ploughed ground at site 389. Grid ref. Centered TL 959 332 map sheet TL93SE Suffolk. Discovered by St Joseph J K, Air Reconnaissance in 1965 (archive record SSF21588), the site is unsigned, unremarked and in the region of four thousand years old. The land remembers.

In the midst of arsenic and tin / April ~~disrumpere~~ reverdie *(at the juncture of a repeating, sumer is icumen in)*; this Middle English text is the title of the 'Cuckoo Song', a medieval rota thought to have been written by W. de Wycombe in the 13th-century.

***Melissomelos*, green after the rain;** Charles Butler (1560–1647), a musician, grammarian, and apiarist wrote, as part of a bee-keeping manual, his first musical score. A notation for voices, it was intended to mimic the sound of bees in 'Melissomelos; The Bees Madrigall' taken from *The Feminine Monarchie: or The Historie of Bees*. The opening verse is reproduced here.

How we make soil or digging a whole; the subheading is excerpted from a quote in a letter from Emily Dickinson to her neighbour, in 1878, and reproduced in *The Letters of Emily Dickinson*. Ed. Thomas H Johnson, Cambridge, MA, Harvard University Press, 1958.

Saxifrage; watching a red tractor working a bluff in Suffolk, with Fin, and then finding meadow saxifrage in its scaldy margins, I was reminded of William Carlos Williams' 'Red Wheelbarrow'. This poem responds to that memory and Williams' imagery.

To come forth from an egg, altricial; Lead-tin yellow was used by Rembrandt in his painting *Belshazzar's Feast* (1636–8), on display at The National Gallery, London. He used this pigment to depict lettering written by the divine hand of God himself, declaring: *"God has numbered the days of your kingdom and brought it to an end; you have been weighed in the balances and found wanting; your kingdom is given to the Medes and Persians."* That night Belshazzar was slain.

Feeding on oak; I remember as a child we were told to count the cuckoo's calls because it called the lengths of our lives.

The dying of an eye; the squirrel study reference in parenthesis is taken from a headline on 3rd March,2022: https://www.technologynetworks.com/ neuroscience/news/

Birching; with two small wings & casting no deep shadow, a birch pioneers; *Piptoporus betulinus*, a mushroom commonly found on birch trees, was discovered carefully packed in the belongings of the Tyrolean Iceman. Archaeologists speculate that it had been used for medicinal purposes.

Brown earth; Argentotype is a manual method (like cyanotype) of image-making which washes the subject in brown (rather than cyan) using a ferrous (iron III-oxide) and silver ion process. The result is known as a Van Dyke brown print after Van Dyke's brown, which is a transparent brown natural earth-based pigment almost entirely comprised of organic matter derived from earthy compounds, such as soil and peat.

How to see angels; the title quote in this poem is excerpted from the preface of *Unquiet Landscape*, by Christopher Neve, Thames & Hudson, 2020. This small piece was inspired by Neve's book.

The way in which light falls; the first line of this poem echoes a phrase found in a letter between John Berger and John Christie in which John writes to John, "*I send you this cadmium red…*" and is the title of a book of correspondence between Berger/Christie published by ACTAR in collaboration with MALM.

A toad strangler of a day; usual a plash / In the plain; the second part of this phrase after the semi-colon from the Celtic poem 'Usual Is the Wind', which appears in the *Red Book of Hergest VI*.

ACKNOWLEDGEMENTS & THANKS

to Tony Frazer for publishing me time and again in *Shearsman* magazine;
for that bedrock there aren't thanks enough;

to Kirsten Norrie for superb editorial care, courage and guidance,
and for warm-hearted support.

to Rebecca Goss for reading the early poems, for steadfast encouragement,
insight and faith in my work.

to Holly Pester for believing in me, for being there from the beginning,
and for loving Fin.

and to James Canton for knowing oaks, this valley and its wildish ways, and for
his support of the ongoing validity in times like these for books such as this.

To the Editors of Muscaliet Press, *Tears in the Fence* and *Fenland Poetry
Journal*, where some of these poems first appeared, and to the Michael Marks
Environmental Poet of the Year 2023/2024 judges for shortlisting some of
these poems in my pamphlet *The Unpinning of Moths*.

Fin, in the green